POETRY FOR

WELL-BEING

Haiku - noun

a Japanese poem of seventeen syllables, in three lines of five, seven, and five, traditionally evoking images of the natural world.

a poem in English written in the form of a haiku.

''Perhaps Haiku might
Kindle thoughts, illuminate
Revealing places'

You are not alone.
Even though it may seem thus;
You. Are. Not. Alone.

For Chris

You are home to me,
Sanctuary and comfort,
Are given with love.

Daughter, wife, mother, wife again, grandmother, employee and 'self-employee'- it's been a full life so far. The ups and downs we all face have kept me busy, but during the pandemic and lockdowns I have had the need to stop, reflect on my life and discover who I am now.

Writing Haiku poetry, in my own way, has become a part of that process, my journey towards healing. I have found Haiku to be both enjoyable and therapeutic, as I whittle the words down, again and again, until just seventeen syllables say exactly what I mean. This book shares some of my poetry and a little of my journey, there is no particular order, and no particular intention, just the sincere hope that some of my words may resonate and you will know that you are not alone.

Grace Daltrey

When I first discovered that I had
issues that needed attention, that I needed counselling,
I found my mind racing, awash with half forgotten mem-
ories, both awake and when asleep. It was exhausting
and frightening, and I couldn't seem to explain it to any-
one else.
Then I discovered the following quote in Horatio Clare's
excellent book about his recovery from psychosis,
'Heavy Light'

'My mind is stuck on subconscious repair'

It spoke to me, told me that he
experienced the same thing as me, and gave the prom-
ise that I wasn't alone. It was most reassuring.

I was prompted to write the next Haiku, based on his
words, and Horatio has kindly given me permission to
use it in this book.

Restless thoughts and dreams,
My mind is on a mission,
Subconscious repair.

修築

repair

Your most important
Relationship, with yourself,
Colours everything.

色彩

colour

You can overcome.
Gather up, unknot your threads,
And be kind to you.

拾う
gather

Inhale then exhale,
Float into serenity,
The calm place, inside.

静か

calm

This moment, this now,
Is everything, all else is
Memories or hope.

想い

hope

Sometimes you'll mess-up,
Console yourself, press onwards,
A better day waits.

将来
future

Just because someone,
Says a thing, doesn't make it
True. Consider your truth.

真理

truth

Broken and damaged was how I used to think about myself. Functioning, but broken in the important ways with no hope of returning to who I used to be.

Now I realise that I will always exist as someone changed by the life I have lived and that I can, and will, change again.

Damaged. But am I?
Beyond repair? Or perhaps,
Simply changed, reborn.

再生
rebirth

The past cannot change,
But it is your foundation,
The place to build from.

下地

foundation

A path to healing;
Seek out the lens that reveals,
The truth of your life.

表す

reveal

Funny that they should
call it comfort eating as
it's anything but.

反語

irony

Gradually I feel,
Moored, authentic again,
It's been a long time.

係留

moored

I'm home. Tears hover,
Gratitude to have, at last,
Arrived at this place.

実家

home

Tattoo on my wrist,
Reminds that I can journey,
To a better now.

旅

journey

Strange thing to observe,
I see others more clearly,
As I mend myself.

治る

heal

Name myself empath,
A lens to focus my life,
Into one story.

表す

focus

You are not tethered,
To the past, loosen your bonds,
Observe and explore.

解く

untie

Shadow walks with me,
Perpetual companion,
Joined, we co-exist.

共存

coexistence

It is a shared road,
Your life, not travelled alone.
The world walks with you.

旅
journey

Your ego and id
should not remain forever
Uncharted terrain.

発見

discover

We get just one life,
So sad to spend it waiting.
Validate yourself.

検証

validate

I'm present again,
In my life. Strange to observe,
That I was mislaid.

現在.

present

Recall your blessings,
Name and count them. Lest they be,
Lost in the whirlwind.

恩惠

blessings

Except for moments,
There is no perfect, it is
unobtainable.

実在

reality

It is imperfect,
This life we live, it does not
Bear close scrutiny.

生命
life

Anxiousness bubbles,
Embrace, accept, breathe. Remain
Right side of alright.

包容

embrace

I've been to that place,
And may return again, but,
I know the road home.

帰る

return

愛を込めて

With love

Printed in Great Britain
by Amazon